READ MY QUIPS

VERN McLELLAN

HARVEST HOUSE PUBLISHERS
Eugene, Oregon 97402

Unless otherwise indicated, all Scripture quotations in this book are taken from The Living Bible, Copyright © 1971 owned by assignment by Illinois Regional Bank N.A. (as trustee). Used by permission of Tyndale House Publishers, Inc., Wheaton, Illinois 60189. All rights reserved.

Verses marked KJV are taken from the King James Version of the Bible.

Verses marked NIV are taken from the Holy Bible, New International Version, Copyright © 1973, 1978, 1984 by the International Bible Society. Used by permission of Zondervan Bible Publishers.

Illustrations by Sandy Silverthorne

READ MY QUIPS

Copyright © 1991 by Vern McLellan
Published by Harvest House Publishers
Eugene, Oregon 97402

Library of Congress Cataloging-in-Publication Data

McLellan, Vernon K.
    Read my quips / Vern McLellan.
    ISBN 0-89081-896-7
    1. American wit and humor.   I. Title.
PN6162.M3475   1991.
818'.5402—dc20   91-14718
                                                            CIP

Printed in the United States of America.

READ MY QUIPS

Contents

In the words of Michel de Montaigne, "I quote others to better express myself." Sir Winston Churchill said, "It's a good thing for an uneducated man to read books of quotations."

"The wisdom of the wise and the experience of the ages are perpetuated by quotations," Benjamin Disraeli declared. "When you take stuff from one writer it's plagiarism," wrote Wilson Mizner, "but when you take it from many writers, it's research."

I'm in the same position as Sir Henry Wotton who wrote, "I am but a gatherer and disposer of other men's stuff." I've been doing this "research" since I was a kid and have loved every minute of it.

Quips and quotes in this book have come from various sources. I've spotted them on moving objects—trikes, trucks, trains, and trolleys. Others came from bumper stickers, restaurant place mats, church bulletins or media communicators who gave no source.

Many jumped out at me from uncopyrighted, homemade publications or were mailed to me by kind friends who, like me, are captivated by thought-provoking—often humorous—one-liners.

Humorist Will Rogers said, "We are all here for a spell; get all the good laughs you can." Don't take life too seriously—you'll never get out of it alive, anyway. In *Read My Quips*, we take a little time to laugh at ourselves. Only in America can we roast our politicians, toast our statesmen, and boast about our national heritage with all its warts and weaknesses. It's still the best thing afloat!

I hope these hundreds of "points of light" will brighten your life, lighten your load, enlighten your mind, and heighten your awareness of and appreciation for those who serve us on so many levels of government. We are so quick to criticize them when they make an error and so slow to compliment when they score in our behalf.

—Vern McLellan
Charlotte, North Carolina

Politics Is Apple Sauce

Politics

I tell you Folks, all Politics is Apple Sauce—*Will Rogers*.

Politics is like football. If you see daylight, go through the hole—*John F. Kennedy*.

Vote for the man who promises least; he'll be the least disappointing—*Bernard Baruch*.

God delights in those who keep their promises, and abhors those who don't—*Solomon* (Proverbs 12:22).

Politics is the most promising of all careers.

In politics, as in love, timing and luck are fundamental—*James Reston*.

Politicians are the same all over. They promise to build a bridge even where there is no river—*Nikita Khrushchev*.

There are two sides to every question, and to hold public office you have to be for both of them.

The keynote in a political campaign is the first one in the scale—"dough"!

At some future time science will find a way to preshrink a politician before election.

Show me a man who sleeps during a political speech and I'll show you a bulldozer.

For years politicians have promised the moon; I'm the first one to be able to deliver it—*Richard M. Nixon*.

If the truth hurts, how come you never see a politician wince?

If exercise removes fat, why do so many politicians have double chins?

A politician is a person who never met a tax he didn't hike.

Most political conventions are like a well-run meat market. You have your choice of baloney.

A politician is someone who says, "A word to the wise is sufficient," then gives a 90-minute speech.

I'll vote for any politician who wouldn't be afraid to have Jack Anderson as his file clerk.

After measuring the candidates, one lamenting voter concluded, "This could be the first primary in history where everybody runs second."

The best thing about this group of candidates is that only one of them can win—*Will Rogers*.

Anyone can win, unless there happens to be a second entry—*George Ade*.

A politician turned to a voter and with pride declared, "I'm a self-made man!"

"Apology accepted," replied the voter.

He who claims to be a self-made man has relieved his Creator of an embarrassing responsibility.

The first requirement of an officeholder is to get reelected.

A principle politicians must accept: When you are right, no one remembers. When you are wrong, no one forgets.

Some people approach every problem with an open mouth—*Adlai Stevenson*.

So live that you wouldn't be ashamed to sell the family parrot to the town gossip—*Will Rogers*.

In war you can be killed only once. In politics, many times—*Winston Churchill*.

Those who like sausage or political policy should not watch it being made.

Winston Churchill was asked why he got into politics. He replied, "Ambition, pure unadulterated ambition."

Then asked what made him stay in politics, "Anger, pure unadulterated anger."

In politics you can often be wrong, but never in doubt.

All politicians should smile—it makes people wonder what they're thinking.

Politicians' political issues are true enough—only their facts have been made up.

Politics ain't worrying this country one-tenth as much as where to find a parking place—*Will Rogers*.

A politician lives a hazardous life. One week he could be featured on the cover of *Time*, the next he could be serving it.

Political Campaign

The hardest thing about any political campaign is how to win without proving that you are unworthy of winning—*Adlai Stevenson*.

The campaign ends Tuesday, but it will take two generations to sweep up the dirt—*Will Rogers*.

I don't want to spend the next two years in Holiday Inns—*Walter Mondale*.

A long-winded political speaker shouted: "What I want is reform. I want tax reform. I want high price reform. I want—I want—"

And a listener cried out: "What you want is chloroform."

Charge and warn, never offer a concrete solution—*Franz Josef Strauss*.

— ★ —

He who slings mud generally loses ground —*Adlai Stevenson*.

— ★ —

A candidate running for Congress hired two assistants: one to dig up the facts and the other to bury them.

— ★ —

If you don't think there is a perfect person in the world, wait until you hear a political campaign speech.

— ★ —

After giving what he considered a stirring, fact-filled campaign speech, the candidate looked out at his audience and confidently asked, "Now, are there any questions?"

"Yes," came a voice from the rear. "Who else is running?"

Political Acrobats

The politician:

★ He's full of promises that go in one year and out the other.

★ He stands for what he thinks people will fall for.

★ He shakes your hand before election and your confidence after.

★ He refuses to answer any questions on the grounds it might eliminate him.

★ Around election time he always announces his views...from his hedgequarters.

★ At the start of a campaign he comes out shooting from the lip.

★ He divides his time between running for office and running for cover.

★ You can count on him to lay down your life for his country.

Most politicians are egotists who have the screaming me-me's.

A political candidate needs five hats: one to wear, one to throw into the ring, one to pass around for donations, one to talk through, and one out of which to pull rabbits!

Contributions

There are two things that are important in politics. The first is money, and I can't remember what the second one is—*Mark Hanna*.

Money is the mother's milk of politics—*Jesse Unruh*.

Money to a politician is like legs to a hockey player. When they go, you're finished—*Bob Perkins*.

If you want to be part of this system, you've got to put your money where your mouth is—*Edward Forgotson*.

Politics has got so expensive that it takes lots of money to even get beat with—*Will Rogers*.

What a political party needs is a cash register with a muffler on it.

Advertising/Publicity

You can fool all of the people some of the time, and some of the people all the time, but you cannot fool all of the people all of the time—*Abraham Lincoln*.

If a man fools me once—shame on him. If the same man fools me twice—shame on me.

You can fool all of the people all of the time if the advertising is right and the budget is big enough—*Joseph Levine*.

The professional politician can sympathize with the professional advertiser. Both must resign themselves to a low public estimation of their veracity and sincerity—*Enoch Powell*.

Advertising men and politicians are dangerous if they are separated. Together they are diabolical —*Philip Adams*.

A good ad should be like a good sermon: It must not only comfort the afflicted—it also must afflict the comfortable—*Bernice Fitz-Gibbon*.

In most of my campaigns, I find it best not to mention my opponent by name because, by doing so it just gives him a chance to get into the headlines—*Harry S. Truman*.

What kills a skunk is the publicity it gives itself —*Abraham Lincoln*.

Media

Journalists do not live by words alone, though sometimes they have to eat them—*Adlai Stevenson*.

The media—mouth organ of the masses.

Absolute silence—that's the one thing a sportswriter can quote accurately—*Indiana basketball coach Bobby Knight*.

A journalist is a grumbler, a censurer, a giver of advice, a regent of sovereigns, a tutor of nations. Four hostile newspapers are more to be feared than a thousand bayonets—*Napoleon*.

A sportswriter is entombed in a prolonged boyhood—*Jimmy Cannon*.

Just why do men lie about each other when the plain truth would be bad enough?

Capitol Punishment

Government

There's no trick to being a humorist when you have the whole government working for you—*Will Rogers*.

Government is...

* ★ a perpetual notion machine.
* ★ another thing that costs more than it's worth.
* ★ a political regime that needs much more pruning and much less grafting.
* ★ an economic system that consists of a few figures followed by many zeros.
* ★ the only organization that operates on a deficit and still makes money.

An elephant is a mouse built to government specifications—*Shortie Long*.

Almost any system of government will work if the people will.

One good reason why a man should get married: He doesn't then have to blame everything on the government.

The less government we have, the better—*Ralph Waldo Emerson*.

The whole art of government consists in being honest—*Thomas Jefferson*.

We all work for the government, but the politician is wise—he gets paid for it.

It's becoming more and more difficult to support the government in the style to which it has become accustomed.

The problem with government is that it often scratches where there ain't no itch.

The strong take from the weak, the rich take from the poor, and the government takes from everyone.

If you want to understand democracy, spend less time in the library with Plato, and more time in the buses with people—*Simeon Strunsky*.

Bureaucracy

Bureaucracy: The people who put in their place the people who put them in their places.

Bureaucracy is based on a willingness either to pass the buck or spend it—*Mrs. Henry J. Serwat*.

There is nothing so permanent as a temporary job in Washington—*George Allen*.

There may now exist great men for things that do not exist—*Jakob Burckhardt*.

Nothing provides more leisure time than a number of capable assistants.

We also serve who only punctuate—*Brian Moore*.

A bureaucrat's idea of cleaning up his files is to make a copy of every paper before he destroys it.

Guidelines for bureaucrats:
1. When in charge ponder.
2. When in trouble delegate.
3. When in doubt mumble.
    —*James H. Boren*

A bureaucrat is a desk jockey—*Dan Bennett*.

There is only one giant machine operated by pygmies, and that is bureaucracy—*Honoré de Balzac*.

— ★ —

The perfect bureaucrat everywhere is the man who manages to make no decisions and escape all responsibility—*Justin Brooks Atkinson*.

— ★ —

[Dealing with bureaucracy] is like trying to nail jelly to the wall—*John F. Kennedy*.

A memorandum is written not to inform the reader but to protect the writer—*Dean Acheson*.

A civil servant is a faceless mortal riding like a flea on the back of the dog, Legislation.

Bureaucrats are the meatloaf of humanity.

If the first person who answers the phone cannot answer your question, it's a bureaucracy—*Lyndon B. Johnson*.

Committees

Outside of traffic, there is nothing that has held this country back as much as committees—*Will Rogers*.

Committee: A group of men who individually can do nothing but as a group decide nothing can be done—*Fred Allen*.

To kill time, a committee is the perfect weapon—*Laurence J. Peter*.

If Moses had been a committee, the Israelites would still be in Egypt—*J.B. Hughes*.

— ★ —

Camel: A horse that was designed by a committee.

— ★ —

Search all the parks
In all of your cities...
You'll find no monuments
To any committees.

— ★ —

If Columbus had had an Advisory Committee he would probably still be at the dock—*Arthur Goldberg*.

— ★ —

Having served on various committees, I have drawn up a list of rules: Never arrive on time; this stamps you as a beginner. Don't say anything until the meeting is half over; this stamps you as being wise. Be as vague as possible; this avoids irritating the others. When in doubt, suggest that a subcommittee be appointed. Be the first to move for adjournment; this will make you popular; it's what everyone is waiting for—*Harry Chapman*.

— ★ —

What is a committee? A group of the unwilling, picked from the unfit, to do the unnecessary —*Richard Harkness*.

Follow the Leaders

Leadership

The trouble with being a leader today is that you can't be sure whether people are following you or chasing you.

A leader is a dealer in hope—*Napoleon*.

The best way to insure support is to involve others.

Remember that it is far better to follow well than to lead indifferently—*John G. Vance*.

A man may lead a horse to the water, but he cannot make it drink.

Let us not look back in anger or forward in fear, but around in awareness—*James Thurber*.

If the blind lead the blind, both shall fall into the ditch—*Jesus* (Matthew 15:14 KJV).

I suppose that leadership at one time meant muscle, but today it means getting along with people—*Indira Gandhi*.

Good fellows are a dime a dozen, but an aggressive leader is priceless—*Red Blaik*.

To be a leader of men one must turn his back on men—*Havelock Ellis*.

Without wise leadership, a nation is in trouble; but with good counselors there is safety—*Solomon* (Proverbs 11:14).

What this country needs are more leaders who know what this country needs.

A real leader faces the music even when he doesn't like the tune—*Arnold H. Glasgow*.

Leadership is the courage to admit mistakes, the vision to welcome change, the enthusiasm to motivate others, and the confidence to stay out of step when everyone else is marching to the wrong tune—*E.M. Estes*.

The best executive is the one who has sense enough to pick good men to do what he wants done, and the self-restraint to keep from meddling with them while they do it—*Theodore Roosevelt*.

The boss drives his men;
   the leader coaches them.
The boss depends upon authority;
   the leader on good will.
The boss inspires fear;
   the leader inspires enthusiasm.
The boss says "I";
   the leader "we."
The boss fixes the blame for the breakdown;
   the leader fixes the breakdown.
The boss says "go";
   the leader says "let's go!"

       —*H. Gordon Selfridge*

He who stands at the head of the line must know where he's going.

Education

If you think education is expensive, try ignorance—*Derek Bok*.

You mustn't enthrone ignorance just because there is so much of it.

Poverty has many roots, but the taproot is ignorance—*Lyndon B. Johnson*.

In a republic, ignorance is a crime. Schoolhouses are the republican line of fortifications—*Horace Mann*.

Give a man a fish, and he will eat for a day. Teach him how to fish, and he will eat for the rest of his life.

If you plan for a decade, plant trees. If you plan for a century, teach the children.

A new graduate rushed out of his college on graduation day and shouted, "Here I am, world. I have my A.B.!"

The world answered, "Sit down, young man, and I'll teach you the rest of the alphabet."

— ★ —

It's a good thing for an uneducated man to read books of quotations—*Winston Churchill.*

— ★ —

Observation more than books, experience rather than persons, are the prime educators—*Amos Bronson Alcott.*

— ★ —

School-days, school-days, dear old
    golden rule days,
Readin' and 'ritin' and 'rithmetic,
Taught to the tune of the hick'ry stick;
You were my queen in calico,
I was your bashful barefoot beau,
And you wrote on my slate, I love you, Joe,
When we were a couple of kids.

—*Will D. Cobb*

— ★ —

A highbrow is a person educated beyond his intelligence—*Brander Matthew.*

There is nothing so stupid as an educated man, if you get off the thing that he was educated in —*Will Rogers*.

— ★ —

We must believe the things we teach our children—*Woodrow Wilson*.

Experience

The taste of defeat has a richness of experience all its own—*Bill Bradley*.

— ★ —

Experience is the name everyone gives to his mistakes.

— ★ —

Ever notice that about the time you think you're to graduate from the school of experience, somebody thinks up a new course?

— ★ —

When I was a boy of fourteen, my father was so ignorant I could hardly stand to have the old man around. But when I got to be twenty-one, I was astonished at how much the old man had learned in seven years—*Mark Twain*.

Experience is a strenuous teacher. No graduates, no degrees, some survivors.

— ★ —

It's best not to be dogmatic; we all make misteaks!

In the Public Eye

Public Officials

A mayor of a city in southern Italy, in an address of welcome to the King of Italy, said, "We welcome you in the name of our 5000 inhabitants, 3000 of whom are in America."

A certain Colonel on the staff of the Governor died suddenly. Many applicants for his position were clamoring to be heard. Before even the funeral had taken place, one of these managed to detain the Governor for a moment, asking, "Would you object to my taking the place of the Colonel?"

"Not at all," snapped the Governor. "Speak to the undertaker."

No man should be in public office who can't make more money in private life—*Thomas E. Dewey.*

When Oliver Cromwell first coined his money, an old cavalier looking on one of the new pieces read this inscription on one side: "God is with us." On the other: "The Commonwealth of England."

"I see," said he, "that God and the Commonwealth are on different sides."

— ★ —

When former Prime Minister Menzies of Australia was sworn into office, various representatives of the press were on hand to interview him. One reporter from the radical press said, somewhat bluntly, "I suppose, Mr. Prime Minister, that you will consult the powerful interests that control you in choosing your Cabinet?"

"Young man," yelped the Prime Minister, "keep my wife's name out of this."

— ★ —

Disraeli, in conversation with a friend, disclosed the secret of his ascendancy in royal favor. "When talking with the Queen," he said, "I observe a simple rule of conduct; I never deny; I never contradict; I sometimes forget."

— ★ —

When you remove dross from silver, you have sterling ready for the silversmith. When you remove corrupt men from the king's court, his reign will be just and fair—*Solomon* (Proverbs 25:4,5).

When you think about having a woman as President, that's no problem. What's worrisome is the thought of having a man for First Lady.

"What do retired U.S. Presidents do?" asked a lady some years ago. "Madam, we spend our time taking pills, and dedicating libraries," explained the venerable expert on the subject, Herbert Hoover.

A young man asked me how I liked being governor. I replied that I liked it. When I go home at night, I sleep like a baby: sleep for an hour and then wake up and cry for an hour—*Winfield Dunn*.

Public officers are the trustees of the people—*Grover Cleveland*.

I would rather be right than president—*Henry Clay*.

You really have to be careful of politicians who have no further ambitions: They may run for the Presidency—*Eugene McCarthy*.

While I'd rather be right than president, at any time I'm ready for both—*Norman Thomas*.

After an all-night meeting between two politicians, eager journalists asked one of them if the meeting was a success.

"Yes, he replied. "We had a real exchange of views. He came in with his and went out with mine."

Doctor: I'm pleased to tell you that you are the father of triplets.

Congressman: Ridiculous. I demand a recount!

Statesman

A statesman is a successful politician who is dead—*Thomas B. Reed*.

A statesman makes the occasion, but the occasion makes the politician—*G.S. Hillard*.

You can always get the truth from an American statesman after he has turned seventy, or given up all hope of the Presidency—*Wendell Phillips*.

When you're abroad you're a statesman; when you're at home you're just a politician—*Sir Harold McMillan.*

A statesman is any politician it's considered safe to name a school after—*Bill Vaughn.*

The difference between a politician and a statesman is: A politician thinks of the next election and a statesman thinks of the next generation—*James F. Clarke.*

The statesman shears the sheep, the politician skins them—*Austin O'Malley.*

He profits most who serves best—*Arthur F. Sheldon.*

Party Politics

The more you read and observe about this Politics thing, you got to admit that each party is worse than the other. The one that's out always looks the best—*Will Rogers.*

The difference between a Republican and a Democrat: One is *in* and the other is *out*.

There's one thing the Democrats and Republicans share in common—our money.

All political parties die at last of swallowing their own lies—*John Arbuthnot*.

[A political] party is organized opinion—*Benjamin Disraeli*.

He serves his party best who serves the country best—*Rutherford B. Hayes*.

The Republicans have their splits right after election and the Democrats have theirs just before an election—*Will Rogers*.

Democrats can't get elected unless things get worse, and things won't get worse unless they get elected—*Jeane Kirkpatrick*.

A bureaucrat is a Democrat who holds some office that a Republican wants—*Alben W. Barkley*.

— ★ —

Nepotism: Appointing your grandmother to office for the good of the party—*Ambrose Bierce*.

Congress

When Edward Everett Hale was Chaplain of the Senate, someone asked him, "Do you pray for the senators, Dr. Hale?"
"No, I look at the senators and pray for the country," he replied.

— ★ —

Congress passes bills and the taxpayers pay them.

— ★ —

Senators are a prolific source of advice, and most of it is bad—*Dean Acheson*.

— ★ —

A Congressman ought to be limited to one term...make him come home and live under the laws he helped pass.

I never got in trouble for what I never said
—*Calvin Coolidge*.

A lot of congressmen and senators like to draw
their breath and their salaries and not do much
else—*Sam Ervin*.

Senate: A club which a hundred men belong to
but pay no dues—*Will Rogers*.

"Congress is so strange," commented Boris Mar-
shalov, a Russian actor and dramatic coach, after a
visit to the spectators' gallery of the House of Representatives. "A man gets up to speak and says
nothing. Nobody listens—and then everyone dis-
agrees."

People ask me where I get my jokes. Why I just
watch Congress and report the facts; I don't even
have to exaggerate—*Will Rogers*.

The country has come to feel the same when
Congress is in session as when the baby gets hold of
a hammer—*Will Rogers*.

Congress fighting inflation is like the mafia fighting crime—*Ray Mossholder*.

I believe if we introduced the Lord's Prayer here...Senators would propose a larger number of amendments to it—*Henry Wilson*.

If "pro" is the opposite of "con," then "progress" is the opposite of "Congress."

The U.S. Senate: An old scow which doesn't move very fast, but never sinks—*Everett Dirksen*.

The Vice President

Did you hear about the man who stepped into the men's room and saw this sign posted over one of the hot-air blowers for drying hands: "Push button and listen for a short message from the Vice President."

Once there were two brothers. One ran away to sea, the other was elected Vice President, and nothing was ever heard of them again—*Thomas R. Marshall*.

The man with the best job in the country is the Vice President. All he has to do is get up every morning and say, "How is the president?"—*Will Rogers*.

— ★ —

The Vice Presidency is...

★ a steppingstone...to oblivion—*Theodore Roosevelt*.

★ a spare tire on the automobile of government —*John Nance Garner*.

★ not such a bad job. All inside work...no heavy lifting—*Walter Mondale*.

★ sort of like the last cookie on the plate. Everyone insists he won't take it, but somebody always does—*Bill Vaughn*.

— ★ —

The Vice President is like a man in a cataleptic state; he cannot speak; he cannot move; he suffers no pain; and yet he is perfectly conscious of everything that is going on around him—*Thomas Marshall*.

Top Dog

Presidents (Quotes by and about...)

The only thing we have to fear is fear itself
—*Franklin D. Roosevelt.*

No one ever listened himself out of a job—*Calvin Coolidge.*

There is one thing about being President—nobody can tell when to sit down—*Dwight D. Eisenhower.*

About Abraham Lincoln:
> A martyr to the cause of man
>   His blood is freedom's eucharist,
> And in the world's great hero list
>   His name shall lead the van.

—*Charles G. Halpin*

Talk to God about me every day by name, and ask him somehow to give me strength for my great task—*Warren G. Harding*.

When a man assumes a public trust, he should consider himself as public property—*Thomas Jefferson*.

Government is like a baby. An alimentary canal with a big appetite at one end and no sense of responsibility at the other—*Ronald Reagan*.

When you get to the end of your rope, tie a knot and hang on—*Franklin D. Roosevelt*.

About Abraham Lincoln: "His heart was as great as the world, but there was no room in it to hold the memory of a wrong"—*Ralph Waldo Emerson*.

Even in the White House one must keep house with himself—*Silas Bent*.

If you can't convince them, confuse them —*Harry S. Truman*.

Tell the truth and you won't have so much to remember—*Abraham Lincoln*.

Doing what's right isn't the problem. It's knowing what's right—*Lyndon B. Johnson*.

Have two goals: wisdom—that is, knowing and doing right—and common sense. Don't let them slip away, for they fill you with living energy, and are a feather in your cap—*Proverbs 3:21,22*.

Nothing in life is so exhilerating as to be shot at without result—*Ronald Reagan* (referring to Winston Churchill's words) after the assassination attempt, March 1981.

When Babe Ruth was asked in 1930 how he felt about making more money than the President of the United States, he replied, "I had a better year than he did!"

When you have got an elephant by the hind leg, and he is trying to run away, it is best to let him go—*Abraham Lincoln*.

I have no expectation of making a hit every time I come to bat—*Franklin D. Roosevelt.*

— ★ —

The buck stops here—*Harry S. Truman.*

— ★ —

It's a recession when your neighbor loses his job; it's a depression when you lose your own—*Harry S. Truman.*

— ★ —

If you can't stand the heat, stay out of the kitchen—*Harry S. Truman.*

— ★ —

I would never read a book if it were possible to talk half an hour with the man who wrote it —*Woodrow Wilson.*

A Stab in the Buck

Inflation

Him: Why do you feel so sorry for the Joneses?
Her: With all this inflation, they can hardly keep up with themselves.

I don't know where the money goes these days. It takes twice as much to live beyond my means as it used to.

Inflation marches on, making it possible for people in all walks of life to live in more expensive neighborhoods without even moving.

"Someone broke into my wife's car," said the man, "and stole $40 worth of groceries—out of the glove compartment."

The tot next door told it like it is: "Mommy's gone to the supermarkup!"

In the old days inflation was just something you did to a balloon or an automobile tire.

Inflation: Being broke with a lot of money in your pocket.

Did you hear about the little boy at the fireworks display who wanted to see the cost of living sky-rocket?

A business executive shopping for a gift for his wife picked out a sweater in a Seattle store and asked, "Could you show me something a bit more expensive?"

The clerk said, "No, but I can put this one away and you could come back in a few days."

Statistics prove that the best time to buy anything is a year ago.

It's tough to pay $2.50 a pound for meat, but it's still tougher to pay less.

Inflation is...

* a crisis in prices.
* a national headache caused by asset indigestion.
* too little for too many for too much.
* a period when it's both the cost and the upcreep.
* a time when your money goes half as far twice as fast.
* the times when the middle class pays upperclass prices.
* the period when it costs a lot more to live beyond your means.
* the period when it costs more to have something repaired than you paid for it originally.
* the period when an ounce of prevention is worth only half a pound of cure.

Sign in bakery: Because of inflation, the name of our pumpernickel bread has been changed to pumperdime.

Inflation is so bad now, I heard a golfer yell "Five!"

Inflation is a shot in the arm that leaves a pain in the neck.

Inflation raises everything but hope.

Inflation is so bad that it has hit the price of feathers. Even down is up.

If this isn't a recession, it must be the worst boom in history.

Why didn't they have the depression when everybody was working?

Things are really rough now. I saw a supermarket with a recovery room.

Fight the rising cost of living—eat at the in-laws!

Inflation: When you never had it so good or parted with it so fast—*Max Hess*.

Two can still live as cheaply as one—if one doesn't show up.

Inflation: A drop in the buck—*Pueblo Pete*.

— ★ —

Inflation is when the buck doesn't stop anywhere.

— ★ —

The way prices keep going up, the next thing we know they'll have the bargain basement on the third floor.

— ★ —

One good thing about inflation is that it's practically impossible for a youngster to get sick on a five-cent candy bar.

— ★ —

Inflation is a stab in the buck.

— ★ —

If inflation continues to soar, you're going to have to work like a dog just to live like one—*George Gobel*.

— ★ —

A nickel ain't worth a dime anymore—*Yogi Berra*.

— ★ —

In the old days a man who saved money was a miser; nowadays he's a wonder.

Life must be worth living—the cost has doubled and still most people hang on.

— ★ —

These days about the only thing you can be sure of getting for a nickel is five pennies.

Till Debt Do
Us Part

The Economy

Economics simplified: When buyers do not fall for prices, prices must fall for buyers.

An economist is a person who can explain clearly what he does not understand.

Stable economy: What you had in the horse-and-buggy days.

An economist is a person who knows a great deal about very little, and who goes along knowing more and more about less and less, until finally he knows practically everything about nothing.

The Dow Jones average is roamin' numerals.

An economist is a man who knows exactly what is going to happen, except he is not quite sure.

Inflation is the most important economic fact of our time—the single greatest peril to our economic health—*Bernard Baruch*.

The secret of economy is to live as cheaply the first few days after payday as you did the last few days before.

Reviewing the economy, did you hear what the ten-year-old boy described as the gross national product? "Spinach!"

Small boy's ambition: I want to grow up to be a farmer so I can get paid for not growing spinach!

Money

Money isn't everything. Sometimes it isn't even enough—*Martha A. Beckman*.

It's not politics that is worrying this country; it's the second payment—*Will Rogers*.

Just be glad you're not getting all the government you're paying for—*Will Rogers.*

The dime isn't entirely worthless; it still makes a pretty good screwdriver.

When we were kids, ten cents was big money—how dimes have changed!

What this country needs is a good five-cent nickel—*Franklin P. Adams.*

The man who saves the pennies is a dandy and a duck—if he always has a quarter for the guy that's out of luck—*Walt Mason.*

Trust in your money and down you go! Trust in God and flourish as a tree!—*Solomon* (Proverbs 11:28).

He who has his thumb on the purse has the power—*Otto von Bismarck.*

When a fellow says, "It ain't the money, but the principle of the thing," it's the money—*Elbert Hubbard*.

The safe way to double your money is to fold it over once and put it in your pocket—*Frank "Kin" Hubbard*.

A stockbroker urged Claude Pepper to buy a stock that would triple in value in a year. Pepper told him, "At my age, I don't even buy green bananas."

Let Wall Street have a nightmare and the whole country has to help get them back in bed again —*Will Rogers*.

If a man's after money, he's money-mad; if he keeps it, he's a capitalist; if he spends it, he's a playboy; if he doesn't get it, he's a ne'er-do-well; if he doesn't try to get it, he lacks ambition. If he gets it without working for it, he's a parasite; and if he accumulates it after a lifetime of hard work, people call him a fool who never got anything out of life —*Victor Oliver*.

Money can't buy friends, but you do get a better class of enemy—*Somers White*.

— ★ —

Don't marry for money; you can borrow it cheaper.

— ★ —

Why do we spend $50,000 on a school bus to haul our children one mile, and then build a $3 million gymnasium for them to get exercise?

— ★ —

About all you can get with a nickel these days is heads or tails.

— ★ —

If a nickel knew what it is worth today, it would feel like two cents.

— ★ —

Son to father, "About my allowance, Pop. It's fallen below the national average for teenagers."

— ★ —

Money may not bring happiness, but most people like to have enough of it around so they can choose their own misery.

He who marries for wealth sells his own liberty.

When someone says "It's only money," it's usually your money he's talking about.

Money used to talk, then it whispered. Now it just sneaks off.

Make all you can, save all you can, give all you can—*John Wesley*.

Most money is tainted. Taint yours and taint mine.

If you make money your god, it will plague you like the devil—*Henry Fielding*.

Debt

Many Americans seem to feel that living within their income is a fate worse than debt.

Blessed are the young, for they shall inherit the national debt—*Herbert Hoover*.

It seems a shame that future generations can't be here to see what wonderful things government is doing with their money.

Is there no way to reverse the trend
    That keeps our country swamped in debt?
Each year we seem to lend and spend
    Money that hasn't been printed yet.
       —*May Richstone*

She who uses charge card to buy hat is in debt over ears.

When we look at the public debt, we're sure posterity will never be out of a job.

Rather go to bed supperless than rise in debt
—*Benjamin Franklin.*

A mortgage casts a shadow on the sunniest field—*Robert Ingersoll.*

— ★ —

The Lord giveth and the landlord taketh away
—*John W. Raper.*

If and when the meek inherit the earth, it looks like they will inherit enough debt to keep them that way.

If you know how to spend less than you get, you have the philosopher's stone.... Beware of little expenses. A small leak will sink a great ship.... Ere you consult your fancy, consult your purse—*Benjamin Franklin*.

Credit

In God we trust, all others pay cash.

Credit: A system of buying on the lay-awake plan.

Creditors have better memories than debtors —*Benjamin Franklin*.

Credit is a system whereby a person who can't pay gets another person who can't pay to guarantee that he can pay—*Charles Dickens*.

You can get about everything on credit now except some good easy money.

A debtor is a man who owes money. A creditor is one who thinks he's going to get it.

Credit cards are what people use after they discover that money can't buy everything.

Budget

If Uncle Sam can't balance his budget, he isn't any smarter than we are.

We'd like to know whether the budget will be balanced by addition or subtraction.

Balancing the budget isn't as bad as budgeting the balance.

— ★ —

Budget: A mathematical confirmation of your suspicions—*A.A. Latimer.*

A budget is...

- ★ something you can stay within only if you go without.
- ★ telling your money where to go instead of wondering where it went.
- ★ a businesslike way to discover that you cannot live within your income.
- ★ a method of saving in which the outcome of the income depends on the outgo of the upkeep.

From the time an infant first tries to get his toes in his mouth, life is a continual struggle to make both ends meet.

Business

We are all manufacturers—some make good, others make trouble, and still others make excuses.

When two men in a business always agree, one of them is unnecessary—*William Wrigley, Jr.*

One of the hardest things about business is minding your own.

A Texas politician waltzed up to the ticket agent at the Dallas-Fort Worth Airport and said, "Ma'am, I'd like you to sell me a first-class ticket."

The agent asked, "But where to, sir?"

The Texan drawled, "It doesn't really matter, ma'am. I've got business all over."

Two acrobats do not dance on the same rope.

Careless merchant—future beggar.

Eat and drink with your relatives; do business with strangers.

There are two times in a man's life when he should not speculate: when he can't afford it, and when he can—*Mark Twain*.

The successful businessman sometimes makes his money by ability and experience, but he generally makes it by mistake—*Owen D. Young*.

Business is like riding a bicycle—either you keep moving or you fall down.

Ten Commandments of Business

1. Handle the hardest job first each day. Easy ones are a pleasure.

2. Do not be afraid of criticism—criticize yourself often.

3. Be happy when the other fellow succeeds—study his methods.

4. Do not be misled by dislikes. Acid ruins the finest fabrics.

5. Be enthusiastic—it's contagious.

6. Do not have the notion that success means simply money-making.

7. Be fair, and do at least one decent act every day of the year.

8. Honor the chief. There must be a head to everything.

9. Have confidence in yourself.

10. Harmonize your work. Let sunshine penetrate and radiate.

The customer is always right—*H. Gordon Selfridge*.

What is good for the country is good for General Motors, and what is good for General Motors is good for the country—*Charles E. Wilson*.

A businessman is judged by the company he keeps solvent.

To err is human—to forgive is not company policy.

Business: What, when you don't have any, you go out of.

Deep in the
Heart of Taxes

Taxes

Another thing I'll never learn,
    Altho it's plain to some, no doubt,
Is why they call it a "return,"
    When all I do is shell it out.
        —Ken Kraft

It's time to pay my income tax
    And, brother, that's no joke.
For after paying IRS
    I find that I R broke!
        —Jerry Henderson

Income tax has made more liars out of the American people than golf has—*Will Rogers*.

The hardest thing in the world to understand is the income tax—*Albert Einstein*.

85

What is the difference between a taxidermist and a tax collector? The taxidermist takes only your skin—*Mark Twain*.

During the tax season, the IRS has special phone numbers. They're for people who like to hear busy signals.

"What's the difference between the short form and the long form?" people keep asking. Well, it's really rather simple. If you use the short form, the government gets the money. If you use the long form, your accountant gets the money!

A lot of people have accountants do their income tax because it saves time. Sometimes 20 years.

The art of taxation consists in so plucking the goose as to get the most feathers with the least hissing—*Jean Baptiste Colbert*.

Next to being shot at and missed, nothing is quite as satisfying as an income tax return—*F.J. Raymond*.

The Eiffel Tower is the Empire State Building after taxes.

Today, it takes more brains and effort to make out the income-tax form than it does to make the income—*Alfred E. Neuman*.

Golf is like taxes—you drive hard to get to the green and then wind up in the hole.

A fine is a tax for doing wrong. A tax is a fine for doing well.

April 15 is the day millions of Americans feel bled, white and blue—*Anna Herbert*.

Title of tax manual: "Gains People Pay"—*Jack Kraus*.

Tax reform means don't tax you,
  don't tax me,
Tax that fellow behind the tree.

—*Russell B. Long*

Father consoling himself: I'm crazy about my kid; let's face it, he's deductible.

The government spends our money,
    And it goes with unseemly haste,
To them it's the Federal Budget—
    To me it's just taxic waste.

The most permanent thing in the world is a temporary tax.

Today the world rotates around its taxes.

Our government could raise unlimited revenue by simply taxing sin.

He who wants to pay less tax should earn less.

Income tax is the fine for reckless thriving.

People who don't pay their taxes in due time, do time.

The biggest challenge Congress faces is to get the money from the taxpayer without disturbing the voter.

— ★ —

Today, a dime is a dollar with all the taxes taken out.

— ★ —

When filing income taxes, it's better to give than to deceive.

— ★ —

If the world is getting smaller, why do they keep raising postal rates?

— ★ —

A tax collector has what it takes to get what you've got.

— ★ —

A government official who gets paid for sticking his nose into other people's business is known as a tax collector.

— ★ —

He who always admires your efforts to improve your lot is a tax assessor.

A tax accountant is a clever man who always saves his client more than enough to pay his fee.

— ★ —

He who is hired to explain that you didn't make the money you did is a tax accountant.

— ★ —

Tax dodger: A man who does not love his country less but loves his money more.

— ★ —

Tax expert: A specialist who, the more he taxes his imagination, the less the government taxes his client.

— ★ —

Tax exemption: A government incentive allowing children to contribute to the support of their parents.

— ★ —

There is just one thing I can promise you about the outer-space program: Your tax dollar will go farther—*Wernher von Braun*.

— ★ —

The trouble with being a breadwinner nowadays is that the Government is in for such a big slice —*Mary McCoy*.

People want *just* taxes more than they want *lower* taxes. They want to know that every man is paying his proportionate share according to his wealth —*Will Rogers*.

We don't seem to be able to check crime, so why not legalize it and then tax it out of business?—*Will Rogers*.

The tax collector must love poor people—he's creating so many of them.

An income tax form is like a laundry list—either way you lose your shirt.

Nothing makes time pass more quickly than an income tax installment every three months.

The reward for saving your money is being able to pay your taxes without borrowing.

An American can consider himself a success when it costs him more to support the government than to support a wife and children.

I'm going to put all my money into taxes. They're sure to go up.

Tax collector: But you are allowed to pay it in quarterly installments.

Taxpayer: I know it, but my heart can't stand it four times a year.

Internal Revenue man, eyeing taxpayer's expense claims: Shall we go over this item-by-item or would you prefer to chicken out right now?

It's hard to believe that America was founded to avoid taxes.

When it comes to paying income taxes, some people think filing means chiseling.

Things could be worse. What if the Tax Office started charging for the tax forms?

I just paid all my taxes, and I'm worried. I still have some money left.

Home: A tax shelter.

— ★ —

Taxation without representation is tyranny
—*James Otis*.

— ★ —

But in this world, nothing is certain but death
and taxes—*Benjamin Franklin*.

— ★ —

Alexander Hamilton originated the put-and-take
system in our national treasury: The taxpayers put
it in, and the politicians take it out—*Will Rogers*.

— ★ —

Johnny swallowed a dime in a store and his
frightened mother called for help. A stranger
promptly seized the squirming boy by the heels,
gave him a few shakes, and the coin rolled out onto
the floor.

The grateful mother thanked the stranger and
asked, "Are you a doctor?"

"No ma'am," he replied. "I work for the IRS."

— ★ —

Folks used to worry because they couldn't take it
with them. In today's tax climate their only worry is
whether it will last as long as they do.

Sign at a service station: We collect taxes—federal, state, local. We also sell gasoline and oil.

The Internal Revenue people know just what to give the man who has everything: an audit!

There is nothing the federal government can give you without taking it away from you first —*Edward R. Annis*.

People who squawk about their income taxes can be divided into two categories: men and women!

Any more taxes, and our take-home pay isn't going to be enough to get us there.

You may not know when you're well off, but the IRS does.

All you have to do to spoil a good day is to figure out how much of your salary will be withheld for taxes.

One taxpayer's lament: I don't want to complain but every time they build a tax structure, the first thing they nail is *me*!

— ★ —

We have a bedbug system of taxation. It's amazing how many different ways they put the bite on you.

— ★ —

An American traveling in the Netherlands met a Hollander who, on learning the traveler's nationality, said, "Our flag is red, white, and blue, too. And when the tax season approaches we begin to feel blue, and when we receive our statements we turn white, and when we pay we see red."

"Yes," replied the American, "but in the United States we see stars as well!"

— ★ —

Government bureau: Where the taxpayer's shirt is kept.

Laying Down
the Law

Law

Let a man keep the law—any law—and his way will be strewn with satisfactions—*Ralph Waldo Emerson*.

No man has ever yet been hanged for breaking the spirit of a law—*Grover Cleveland*.

Laws are not masters but servants, and he rules them who obeys them—*Henry Ward Beecher*.

I did not become a president to preside over mounting violence and deepening disorder—*Lyndon B. Johnson*. (This is a paraphrase of Winston Churchill: "I have not become the King's First Minister in order to preside over the liquidation of the British Empire.")

Laws too gentle are seldom obeyed; too severe, seldom executed—*Benjamin Franklin*.

No man is above the law and no man is below it; nor do we ask any man's permission when we require him to obey it—*Theodore Roosevelt*.

Justice

Children are innocent and love justice, while most adults are wicked and prefer mercy—*G.K. Chesterton*.

Corn can't expect justice from a court composed of chickens—*African proverb*.

Justice tempered with too much mercy becomes injustice.

Those who chronically suffer injustice have the truest insight into what justice is all about.

One mouse eats the clothes and all the mice get into trouble.

You should defend those who cannot help themselves. Yes, speak up for the poor and helpless and see that they get justice—*Lemuel* (Proverbs 31:8,9).

Judgment

There is so much good in the worst of us,
  And so much bad in the best of us,
That it hardly becomes any of us
  To talk about the rest of us.

— ★ —

E'er you remark another's sin,
  Bid your own conscience look within.

—*Benjamin Franklin*

— ★ —

Cruel and cold is the judgment of man,
  Cruel as winter, and cold as the snow;
But by-and-by will the deed and the plan
  Be judged by the motive that lieth below.

—*Lewis J. Bates*

— ★ —

Four things belong to a judge: to hear courteously, to answer wisely, to consider soberly, and to decide impartially—*Socrates*.

If you want favor with God and man, and a reputation for good judgment and common sense, then trust the Lord completely; don't ever trust yourself—*Solomon* (Proverbs 3:4,5).

If I was as bad as they say I am,
  And you were as good as you look,
I wonder which one would feel the worst
  If each for the other was took?

  —*George Barr Baker*

It is therefore that the older I grow, the more apt I am to doubt my own judgment, and to pay more respect to the judgment of others—*Benjamin Franklin*.

Forbear to judge, for we are sinners all—*William Shakespeare*.

The man who knows right from wrong and has good judgment and common sense is happier than the man who is immensely rich! For such wisdom is far more valuable than precious jewels. Nothing else compares with it—*Solomon* (Proverbs 3:13-15).

Wisdom

Before God we are equally wise—equally foolish—*Albert Einstein*.

Wisdom is the child of experience—*John F. Kennedy*.

Nine-tenths of wisdom is being wise in time —*Theodore Roosevelt*.

We must all hang together, or assuredly we shall all hang separately—*Benjamin Franklin*.

Half-heartedness never won a battle—*William McKinley*.

Faith in God is meant to be bread for daily use, not cake for special occasions.

A wise man is like a pin; his head keeps him from going too far.

I would rather be the man who bought the Brooklyn Bridge than the one who sold it—*Will Rogers.*

The wise are promoted to honor, but fools are promoted to shame!—*Solomon* (Proverbs 3:35).

He who is a wise man by day is no fool by night.

Wise men change their minds, fools never.

God grant me the serenity to accept the things I cannot change; the courage to change the things I can; and the wisdom to know the difference —*Reinhold Niebuhr.*

The wisest man remembers that to catch a mouse you starve a cat.

If you want to know what God wants you to do, ask him, and he will gladly tell you, for he is always ready to give a bountiful supply of wisdom to all who ask him; he will not resent it—*James* (James 1:5).

As a man grows wiser, he talks less and says more.

Some men are wise, and some are otherwise.

He who loves wisdom loves his own best interest and will be a success—*Solomon* (Proverbs 19:8).

Wisdom in the man, patience in the wife, bring peace to the house, and a happy life.

Common Sense

But no, that would be common sense—and out of place in a government—*Mark Twain*.

Common sense is in spite of, not the result of, education.

Common sense is the sixth sense (though not as common as it used to be), given to us by God to keep the other five from making fools of themselves—and us.

Just because it's common sense, doesn't mean it's common practice—*Will Rogers*.

— ★ —

A handful of common sense is worth a bushel of learning—*Spanish proverb*.

— ★ —

Common sense in an uncommon degree is what the world calls wisdom—*Samuel T. Coleridge*.

— ★ —

Getting wisdom is the most important thing you can do! And with your wisdom, develop common sense and good judgment—*Solomon* (Proverbs 4:7).

— ★ —

Have two goals: wisdom—that is, knowing and doing right—and common sense. Don't let them slip away, for they fill you with living energy, and bring you honor and respect. They keep you safe from defeat and disaster and from stumbling off the trail. With them on guard you can sleep without fear; you need not be afraid of disaster or the plots of wicked men, for the Lord is with you; he protects you—*Solomon* (Proverbs 3:21-26).

Red...or Red, White, and Blue?

Communism

A communist is like a crocodile—when it opens its mouth you cannot tell whether it is trying to smile or preparing to eat you up—*Winston Churchill.*

Communism boasts of putting a new suit on every man. Christianity promises to place a new man in every suit.

The theory of communism may be summed up in one sentence: Abolish all private property—*Karl Marx.*

Free speech isn't dead in Russia—only the speakers.

The commissar traveled over from Moscow to one of the farming communes for a firsthand report.

"Comrade," he bellowed to one of the nearby peasants, "I keep hearing bad stories. *You* tell me. How is the potato crop this year?"

Ivan, the peasant, stroked his chin a few times, then remarked, "Actually, we've got a pile of potatoes that'll reach to the pearly gates of heaven!"

"Ahhh," the Commissar began, "that's more like it." Then he stopped short. "What do you mean? There is no heaven."

Said Ivan dryly, "And there are no potatoes, either!"

The Commissar didn't laugh. Within moments Ivan was about to be shipped off to Siberia. Ivan, always the optimist, decided to plea-bargain: "Sir, I've got an idea. Why exile me to Siberia? It's part of our Soviet state, so it cannot be all bad."

"What do you have in mind?" the Commissar demanded.

"Well, since childhood I've been hearing that the United States is the absolute worst place on the earth. Why not send me there as punishment instead?"

Nobody laughed that time either.

— ★ —

"Have you heard the news? *Pravda* is going to hold a competition for the best political joke."

"What's the first prize?"

"Twenty years!"

"What's the definition of a string quartet?"
"The Leningrad Symphony just back from a Western tour."

Russia has abolished God but so far God has been more tolerant—*John Cameron Swayze*.

America

America: Where there are ten million laws to enforce the Ten Commandments.

America: Where a man can say what he thinks, if he isn't afraid of his wife, his boss, his customer, his neighbors, or the government.

In America there are two classes of travel: first class, and with children—*Robert Benchley*.

America: A land where we can say what we think even without thinking.

An American woman who respects herself must buy something every day of her life—*Henry James*.

The trouble with this country is that there are too many people going around saying, "The trouble with this country is..."—*Sinclair Lewis*.

— ★ —

Keep the commandments and keep your life; despising them means death—*Solomon* (Proverbs 19:16).

— ★ —

All in all, America is a most incredible country—laced with controversies and inconsistencies, yes, but an amazing, wonderful place to live.

The nation's condition is remindful of two little boys walking home from Sunday school. They were discussing the lesson of the day. Alvin, the most vocal, kept making fun of Noah: "Just think what it was like with all those animals and snakes and things. It was so crowded. The noise must have been horrible all the time. They had to feed 'em, too—even the birds flying around all over the place. And the smell—yeeech!"

Johnny listened awhile, then finally stopped the conversation. "Yeah," he said, "but think about it. It was still the best thing afloat!"

— ★ —

How little do my countrymen know what precious blessings they are in possession of, and which no other people on earth enjoy—*Thomas Jefferson*.

America is great because America is good, and if America ever ceases to be good, America will cease to be great—*Alexis de Tocqueville*.

— ★ —

The thing that impresses me most about America is the way parents obey their children—*Duke of Windsor*.

— ★ —

Let America realize that self-scrutiny is not treason. Self-examination is not disloyalty—*Richard Cardinal Cushing*.

— ★ —

Whatever America hopes to bring to pass in the world must first come to pass in the heart of America—*Dwight D. Eisenhower*.

— ★ —

All America has to do to get in bad all over the world is just to start out on what we think is a Good Samaritan mission—*Will Rogers*.

— ★ —

A churchless community, a community where men have abandoned and scoffed at or ignored their religious needs, is a community on the rapid downgrade—*Theodore Roosevelt*.

The overwhelming majority of Americans are possessed by two great qualities—a sense of humor and a sense of proportion—*Franklin D. Roosevelt.*

American: One who will cheerfully respond to every appeal except to move back in the bus.

America is a country that doesn't know where it is going but is determined to set a speed record getting there—*Laurence J. Peter.*

Americans are like a rich father who wishes he knew how to give his sons the hardships that made him rich—*Robert Frost.*

Americans: People who laugh at . . . African witch doctors and spend $100 million on fake reducing systems—*Leonard Levinson.*

History fails to record a single precedent in which nations subject to moral decay have not passed into political and economic decline. There has been either a spiritual awakening to overcome the moral lapse, or a progressive deterioration leading to ultimate national disaster—*Douglas MacArthur.*

Godliness exalts a nation, but sin is a reproach to any people—*Solomon* (Proverbs 14:34).

Those who cannot remember the past are condemned to repeat it—*George Santayana*.

Only good men enjoy life to the full; evil men lose the good things they might have had, and they themselves shall be destroyed—*Solomon* (Proverbs 2:21,22).

We cannot survive as a free nation when some men decide that others are not fit to live and should be abandoned to abortion or infanticide —*Ronald Reagan*.

We don't know what we want, but we are ready to bite somebody to get it—*Will Rogers*.

It has often been asked what this nation stands for, and the answer is easy—too much.

Whoever wants to know the hearts and minds of America had better learn baseball—*Jacques Barsun*.

America is a large, friendly dog in a small room. Everytime it wags its tail it knocks over a chair
—*Arnold Toynbee.*

— ★ —

The trouble with the American public is that it thinks something is better than nothing—*Alfred Stieglitz.*

— ★ —

Our national flower is the concrete cloverleaf
—*Lewis Mumford.*

Land of Opportunity

An American is a fellow wearing English tweeds, a Hong Kong shirt and Spanish shoes, who sips Brazilian coffee sweetened with Philippine sugar, from a Bavarian cup while nibbling on Swiss cheese, sitting at a Danish desk over a Persian rug, after coming in a German car from an Italian movie...and takes advantage of the opportunity to write his congressman with a Japanese ballpoint pen on French paper, demanding that he do something about foreigners taking away our foreign markets.

— ★ —

The doors of opportunity are marked "Push" and "Pull."

A wise man will make more opportunities than he finds—*Francis Bacon.*

— ★ —

He who is looking for opportunities will find them dressed in work clothes.

— ★ —

Between tomorrow's dream and yesterday's regret is today's opportunity.

Thanksgiving

So once in every year we throng
   Upon a day apart,
To praise the Lord with feast and song
   In thankfulness of heart.

         —Arthur Guiterman

— ★ —

Ah! on Thanksgiving day, when from East
   and from West,
From North and South, come the pilgrim
   and guest...
What moistens the lip and what brightens the eye?
What calls back the past, like the rich pumpkin
   pie?

         —John Greenleaf Whittier

Thanksgiving Day . . . the one day that is purely American—*O. Henry*.

— ★ —

On Thanksgiving Day all over America, families sit down to dinner at the same moment—halftime.

— ★ —

General Carlos P. Romulo, a Philippine general, lived in the United States for 17 years. As he was about to return to his homeland, he gave this farewell statement:

"Never forget, America, that yours is a spiritual country. Yes, I know you're a practical people and, like others, I have marveled at your factories and skyscrapers and your arsenals. But underlying everything else is the fact that America began as a God-loving, God-fearing, and God-worshiping people. It is this spirit that makes America invincible. May God keep you always, and may you always keep God."

The Proverbial Rat Race

Life is a rat race and the rats are winning.

— ★ —

I don't know if I'm slowing up or they're bringing in faster rats!—*Robert Orben*.

The trouble with the rat race is that even if you win, you're still a rat—*Lily Tomlin.*

— ★ —

The rat race being what it is, I could use a little more cheese each week—*Salo.*

— ★ —

I often feel I'll just opt out of this rat race and buy another hunk of Utah—*Robert Redford.*

— ★ —

When they ask me about Race in a question-naire, I always put down Rat.

By the Book

The Bible in National Life

It is impossible to rightly govern the world without God and the Bible—*George Washington*.

— ★ —

In this Book will be found the solution of all the problems of the world—*Calvin Coolidge*.

— ★ —

Most people are bothered by those passages of Scripture they do not understand, but the passages that bother me are those I *do* understand—*Mark Twain*.

— ★ —

I believe the Bible is the best gift God has ever given to man. All the good from the Savior of the world is communicated to us through this book —*Abraham Lincoln*.

Despise God's Word and find yourself in trouble. Obey it and succeed—*Solomon* (Proverbs 13:13).

Men do not reject the Bible because it contradicts itself but because it contradicts them.

The Bible is worth all other books which have ever been printed—*Patrick Henry*.

That book, sir, is the rock on which our republic rests—*Andrew Jackson*.

In all my perplexities and distresses, the Bible has never failed to give me light and strength —*Robert E. Lee*.

Sin will keep you from this book. This book will keep you from sin—*Dwight L. Moody*.

Nobody ever outgrows Scripture; the Book widens and deepens with our years—*Charles Spurgeon*.

The Bible is criticized most by those who read it least.

— ★ —

The Bible is the sheet-anchor of our liberties —*Ulysses Grant*.

— ★ —

Get the most out of the Bible: Read it through; pray it in; work it out; note it down; and pass it on.

— ★ —

The Bible is no mere book, but a Living Creature, with a power that conquers all that oppose it—*Napoleon*.

— ★ —

Other books were given for our information; the Bible was given for our transformation.

— ★ —

When you read the Bible and see a "therefore," try to discover what it is there for.

Prayer

Note on high-school bulletin board: In the event of nuclear attack all bans on prayer in this school will be lifted.

I have been driven many times to my knees by the overwhelming conviction that I had nowhere else to go. My own wisdom, and that of all about me seemed insufficient for the day—*Abraham Lincoln*.

Life is fragile, handle with prayer.

O, do not pray for easy lives. Pray to be stronger men. Do not pray for tasks equal to your powers. Pray for powers equal to your tasks—*Phillips Brooks*.

Prayer should be the key of the day and the lock of the night—*Thomas Fuller*.

Men who are strangers to prayer are strangers to power.

Satan trembles when he sees the weakest saint upon his knees—*William Cowper*.

The quickest way to get back on your feet is to get down on your knees.

Pray without ceasing—*Paul* (1 Thessalonians 5:17 KJV).

Men ought always to pray and not to faint —*Luke*, paraphrasing Jesus (Luke 18:1 KJV).

More things are wrought by prayer than this world dreams of—*Alfred Lord Tennyson*.

Then if my people will humble themselves and pray, and search for me, and turn from their wicked ways, I will hear from heaven and forgive their sins and heal their land—*the Lord*, speaking to Solomon (2 Chronicles 7:14).

He who ceases to pray ceases to prosper—*W.G. Benham*.

It is not well for a man to pray cream and live skim milk—*Henry Ward Beecher*.

— ★ —

I have lived to thank God that all my prayers have not been answered—*Jean Ingelow*.

Pray as if everything depended upon God and work as if everything depended upon man—*Frances Cardinal Spellman.*

— ★ —

Call on God, but row away from the rocks —*Indian proverb.*

My Country 'Tis of Thee

Patriotism

Ask not what your country can do for you: Ask what you can do for your country—*John F. Kennedy*.

"Our country right or wrong." When right to be kept right. When wrong to be put right—*Carl Schurz*.

Patriotism is easy to understand in America; it means looking out for yourself by looking out for your country—*Calvin Coolidge*.

Breathes there the man with soul so dead,
    Who never to himself hath said,
This is my own, my native land!
          —*Walter Scott*

A man's feet must be planted in his country, but his eyes should survey the world—*George Santayana*.

I only regret that I have but one life to give for my country—*Nathan Hale*.

National enthusiasm is the great nursery of genius.

Duty

A man who neglects his duty as a citizen is not entitled to his rights as a citizen—*Tiorio*.

A duty dodged is like a debt unpaid; it is only deferred, and we must come back and settle the account at last—*Joseph F. Newton*.

It is the duty of government to make it difficult for people to do wrong, easy to do right—*William E. Gladstone*.

I slept, and dreamed that life was Beauty;
I woke and found that life was Duty.

The best way to get rid of your duties is to discharge them.

— ★ —

Duties are the tasks we look forward to with distaste, perform with reluctance, and brag about ever after.

— ★ —

A sentry on guard duty for the first time had orders not to admit any car unless it had a special identification seal. A general rode in the first unmarked car the sentry stopped. When the general told his driver to go right through, the sentry politely said, "I'm new at this, sir. Who do I shoot first, you or the driver?"

— ★ —

When duty calls, some people are never at home.

— ★ —

Duty without enthusiasm becomes laborious; duty with enthusiasm becomes glorious—*William A. Ward.*

— ★ —

You [Americans] have enormous reserves and vitality, but this also means that you have duties —*Former West German Chancellor Helmut Schmidt.*

Once you pledge, don't hedge—*Nikita Khrushchev*.

Involvement

The United States is a country of quiet majorities and vociferous minorities.

The only thing necessary for the triumph of evil is for good men to do nothing—*Edmund Burke*.

Bad officials are elected by good citizens who do not vote—*George Jean Nathan*.

The good influence of godly citizens causes a city to prosper, but the moral decay of the wicked drives it down—*Solomon* (Proverbs 11:11).

The people who are the most bigoted are the people who have no convictions at all—*G.K. Chesterton*.

Whatever makes men good Christians makes them good citizens—*Daniel Webster*.

There is no group in America that can withstand the force of an aroused public opinion—*Franklin D. Roosevelt*.

I am only one, but I am one. I cannot do everything, but I can do something. And because I cannot do everything, I will not refuse to do the something that I can do—*Edward Everett Hale*.

If we ever pass out as a nation we ought to put on our tombstone, "America died from a delusion that she had moral leadership"—*Will Rogers*.

With good men in authority, the people rejoice; but with the wicked in power, they groan—*Solomon* (Proverbs 29:2).

It is not the man who sits by his fireside reading his evening paper, and saying how bad are politics and politicians, who will ever do anything to save us; it is the man who goes out into the rough hurly-burly of the caucus, the primary, and the political meeting, and there faces his fellows on equal terms—*Theodore Roosevelt*.

First inebriate: Tell me, what's *ignorance* and what's *apathy?*

Second inebriate: *I don't know* and *I don't care.*

I urge, then, first of all, that requests, prayers, intercession and thanksgiving be made for everyone—for kings and all those in authority, that we may live peaceful and quiet lives in all godliness and holiness—*Paul* (1 Timothy 2:1,2 NIV).

I would like to see every true believer involved in politics in some way, shape, or form—*Billy Graham.*

Where's the manly spirit of the truehearted and the unshackled gone? Sons of old freemen, do we but inherit their names alone? Is the old pilgrim spirit quench'd within us? Stoops the proud manhood of our souls so low that mammon's lure or party's wile can win us to silence now? Now, when our land to ruin's brink is verging, in God's name let us speak while there is time: now, when the padlock for our lips is forging, silence is a crime —*John Greenleaf Whittier.*

Voting

Where annual elections end, there slavery begins—*John Quincy Adams.*

The future of this republic is in the hands of the American voter—*Dwight D. Eisenhower.*

A straw vote only shows which way the hot air blows—*O. Henry.*

We preach the virtues of democracy abroad. We must practice its duties here at home. Voting is the first duty of democracy—*Lyndon B. Johnson.*

The mandate of November's election must be by the vote of the people—not by default of the people—*Lyndon B. Johnson.*

The secret ballot in America is the most sacred heritage which we have and that I have stood by. Even my wife doesn't know how I voted—*Nelson A. Rockefeller.*

The number one problem in our country is apathy—but no one seems to care!

When you have to make a choice and don't make it, that in itself is a choice—*William James.*

Among free men there can be no successful appeal from the ballot to the bullet....The ballot is stronger than the bullet—*Abraham Lincoln*.

An American will cross the ocean to fight for democracy, but won't cross the street to vote in a national election.

The Velvet Touch

Diplomacy

Diplomats should emulate musicians who never conduct foreign overtures without knowing the score.

Diplomacy: The business of handling a porcupine without disturbing the quills.

I wish there were some giant economy-size aspirin tablet that would work on international headaches. But there isn't. The only cure is patience with reason mixed in—*Lyndon B. Johnson*.

Diplomats are useful only in fair weather. As soon as it rains they drown in every drop—*Charles de Gaulle*.

A diplomat is someone who...

* ★ thinks twice before saying nothing.
* ★ has the knack of making a point without making an enemy.
* ★ can bring home the bacon without spilling the beans.
* ★ prefers ironing out his differences to flattening his opponent.
* ★ remembers a woman's birthday but forgets her age.
* ★ can be disarming even though his country isn't.
* ★ can juggle a hot potato long enough for it to become a cold issue.
* ★ says "I will take the matter under advisement," instead of "No."
* ★ is long on protocol and short on memory.
* ★ is appointed to interfere in the affairs of others.
* ★ has to watch his appease and accuse.
* ★ can tell another person where to go so pleasantly that he's eager to start.
* ★ sometimes speaks his mind, but more often minds his speech.
* ★ may not be musical but knows when to soft-pedal.
* ★ can yawn with his mouth closed.
* ★ has the art of letting someone else have his own way.

Let us never negotiate out of fear. But let us never fear to negotiate—*John F. Kennedy*.

Diplomacy is the art of saying "nice doggie" until you can find a rock.

A distinguished diplomat can hold his tongue in ten languages.

When diplomats say they agree in principle, it means that in ten years the issue will be settled.

The art of diplomacy, especially in this atomic age, must lead to peace, not war or the brink of war—*Adlai Stevenson*.

It is never too early to try; it is never too late to talk; and it is high time that many disputes on the agenda of this Assembly were taken off the debating schedule and placed on the negotiating table —*John F. Kennedy*.

Diplomacy is to do and say the nastiest thing in the nicest way—*Isaac Goldberg*.

After four years at the United Nations, I sometimes yearn for the peace and tranquillity of a political convention—*Adlai Stevenson*.

War

In war, there is no second prize for the runner-up—*Omar Bradley*.

War does not determine who is right—only who is left.

It is well that war is terrible—we would grow too fond of it—*Robert E. Lee*.

In peace, sons bury their fathers; in war, fathers bury their sons—*Herodotus*.

There are no atheists in the foxholes—*William Thomas Cummings*.

The whole art of war consists of guessing at what is on the other side of the hill—*Duke of Wellington*.

War is mainly a catalogue of blunders—*Winston Churchill*.

War would end if the dead could return—*Stanley Baldwin*.

War is much too important a matter to be left to the generals—*Georges Clemenceau*.

Sometime they'll give a war and nobody will come—*Carl Sandburg*.

Future

My interest is in the future because I'm going to spend the rest of my life there.

The best thing about the future is that it comes only one day at a time.

The trouble with our times is that the future is not what it used to be—*Paul Valéry*.

The future is history with God, for He knows all things.

Nowadays a man often goes into politics with a wonderful future and comes out with a terrible past.

Owing to unforeseen circumstances, our course entitled "Predicting Your Future" has had to be canceled.

I resolve to be optimistic about the future—if there is one.

The future belongs to those who prepare for it.

The wise man saves for the future, but the foolish man spends whatever he gets—*Solomon* (Proverbs 21:20).

— ★ —

Your future is as bright as the promises of God.

— ★ —

Hats off to the past, sleeves up for the future.

— ★ —

A prudent man foresees the difficulties ahead and prepares for them; the simpleton goes blindly on and suffers the consequences—*Solomon* (Proverbs 22:3).

— ★ —

I have known personal disappointments and despair. But always the thought of tomorrow has buoyed me up. I have looked to the future all my life. I still do. I still believe that with courage and intelligence we can make the future bright with fulfillment—*Bernard Baruch*.

— ★ —

If we open a quarrel between the past and the present, we shall find we have lost the future —*Winston Churchill*.

Here lies my past,
  Good-bye I have kissed it;
Thank you, kids,
  I wouldn't have missed it.

—*Ogden Nash*

I tell you the past is a bucket of ashes—*Carl Sandburg*.

The greatest use of life is to spend it for something that will outlast it—*William James*.

You fall the way you lean.

Where you go hereafter depends on *what* you go after here.

Index

Index

154

Other Harvest House Books by Vern McLellan

PROVERBS FOR PEOPLE
by *Vern McLellan*

Clever proverbs are matched with a corresponding
Scripture reference and illustration that will bring
a smile and a cause for reflection with the turn of
each page.

SHREDDED WIT
by *Vern McLellan*

Crisp, crackling, popping-good one liners from the
author of *Proverbs for People* and *Quips, Quotes, and
Quests*. A "bran" new serving of insightful bitefuls
of wit and wisdom. Supplement your diet with
hundreds of delightful and inspirational morsels of
high fiber humor. Over 100,000 Vern McLellan
books now in print!

WISE WORDS FROM A WISE GUY
by *Vern McLellan*

Back with his latest collection of the wise and
wacky, master wordsmith Vern McLellan is ready to
brighten your life and conversation with illustrated
principles and humor based on the sayings of
Solomon and others.

Filled with a multitude of conversation-starters,
quick comebacks, and inspirational morsels
delightfully illustrated by Sandy Silverthorne, *Wise
Words from a Wise Guy* is a perfect gift—for yourself
or a friend—with a wisdom-filled message!

LOVE LINES
by *Vern McLellan*

Love Lines takes a look at the light side of romance, but is loaded with practical advice from God's Word as well. A perfect gift to help keep romance in your relationship.

CREAM OF WIT
by *Vern McLellan*

This "cream of the crop" collection of quips, quotes, and anecdotes will sharpen your mind and quicken your step. *Cream of Wit* is perfect for students and teachers, writers and preachers— anyone who enjoys scrumptious one-liners.

For information on how to purchase any of Vern McLellan's books, contact your local bookstore or send a self-addressed stamped envelope to:

Mission Services
P.O. Box 2021
Charlotte, NC 28247-6021